The Three Wise Women

Other Crossway books by
CHRISTIN DITCHFIELD

A Family Guide to Narnia

Take It To Heart

*A Family Guide to
The Lion, the Witch and the Wardrobe*

CHRISTIN DITCHFIELD

THE

3 Wise
Women

A CHRISTMAS REFLECTION

CROSSWAY BOOKS
WHEATON, ILLINOIS

Cover design: Josh Dennis

Cover and Interior illustrations: Bernhard Oberdieck

First printing, 2005

Printed in the United States of America

All Scripture quotations, unless otherwise indicated, are taken from *The Holy Bible: New International Version.* Copyright © 1973, 1978, 1984 by International Bible Society. Used by permission of Zondervan Publishing House. All rights reserved. The "NIV" and "New International Version" trademarks are registered in the United States Patent and Trademark Office by International Bible Society. Use of either trademark requires the permission of International Bible Society.

Scripture quotations indicated as from ESV are taken from *The Holy Bible: English Standard Version,*® copyright © 2001 by Crossway Bibles, a publishing ministry of Good News Publishers. Used by permission. All rights reserved.

Scripture quotations indicated as from KJV are taken from the King James Version.

Scripture quotations indicated as from NLT are taken from *The Holy Bible: New Living Translation,* copyright © 1996. Used by permission of Tyndale House Publishers, Inc., Wheaton, Illinois 60189. All rights reserved.

Library of Congress Cataloging-in-Publication Data
Ditchfield, Christin
   Three wise women : a Christmas reflection / Christin
Ditchfield.
     p. cm.
   Includes bibliographical references.
   ISBN 13: 978-1-58134-636-7 (hc : alk. paper)
   ISBN 10: 1-58134-636-0
   1. Christian women—Prayer-books and devotions—English.
2. Mary, Blessed Virgin, Saint—Meditations. 3. Elizabeth
(Mother of John the Baptist), Saint—Meditations. 4. Anna
(Biblical prophetess)—Meditations. 5. Jesus Christ—Nativity—
Meditations. I. Title.
BV4844.D58   2005
232.91—dc22   2005003641

LB		15	14	13	12	11	10	09	08	07
15	14	13	12	11	10	9	8	7	6	5	4	3	2

This book is lovingly dedicated to three truly wise women, whose godly examples have inspired me all of my life—each in their own unique way:

My mother and best friend,
Bernice

and my precious grandmothers,
Joan Ditchfield and Doris Roberts

Contents

Introduction

Now when Jesus was born in Bethlehem of Judea
in the days of Herod the king, behold, there came
wise men from the east to Jerusalem, saying,
Where is he that is born King of the Jews?
for we have seen his star in the east, and are come
to worship him. . . . And, lo, the star, which they saw
in the east, went before them, till it came and
stood over where the young child was.
When they saw the star, they rejoiced with
exceeding great joy . . . they saw the young child
with Mary his mother, and fell down and
worshipped him: and when they had opened
their treasures, they presented unto him gifts;
gold, and frankincense, and myrrh.

MATTHEW 2:1-2, 9-11, KJV

ver the years these men have come to
be known as Gaspar, Melchior, and Balthasar—the
three Wise Men—beloved characters in the tradi-

tional Christmas story. Though they are mentioned only briefly in the Gospel of Matthew, the Wise Men appear in nearly every Nativity scene, every crèche. Their images adorn greeting cards and ornaments. Countless songs, stories, and poems have been written about them. Somehow, through the centuries these mysterious figures have captured our imagination and inspired us to "follow the star" on our own spiritual journey to Bethlehem.

Of course we don't really know what their names were, or even that there were in fact three of them. We assume that there must have been at least three, because there were three gifts. However, if we read the Gospel accounts of the Christmas story carefully, we soon discover that there certainly were three wise people—three Wise Women.

Mary, Elizabeth, and Anna were three very different women, in different ages and stages of life.

One single, one married, one widowed. One just beginning to experience life, one coping with the challenges and changes of midlife, and one coming close to the end of life.

How do we know they were wise? The Scripture tells us, "The fear of the LORD is the beginning of wisdom: and knowledge of the Holy is understanding" (Proverbs 9:10, KJV). All three of these women feared the Lord. They were women who walked with Him. Women of faith and courage and character.

Each one played a crucial role in the events of the true Christmas story. Mary became the mother of the Messiah. She gave birth to the Son of God Himself. Elizabeth became the mother of His prophet, John. She also served as Mary's mentor and confidante. Anna announced the newborn King's arrival. She sang His praises and proclaimed His salvation to all who had ears to hear.

Too often we casually read over the familiar

words of Scripture, barely noticing these women. Yet each one, in her own way, set a powerful example for us to follow today. If we want to learn what these Wise Women have to teach us, we must take a closer look and see what their stories reveal about their hearts.

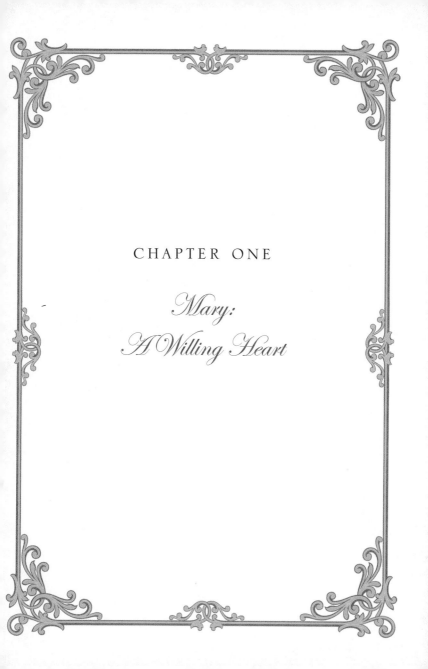

CHAPTER ONE

Mary:
A Willing Heart

1

Mary: A Willing Heart

Behold the handmaid of the Lord;
be it unto me according to
thy word.

LUKE 1:38, KJV

For centuries scholars, theologians, artists, musicians, and poets have contemplated the mystery of the virgin birth and have tried to answer this haunting question: What was so special about the girl from Nazareth, the young woman called Mary? Why did God choose her—above all the other women on earth—to be the mother of His only begotten Son? Was it the purity of her heart? Or the depth of her devotion to Him?

Did she have the perfect personality? Or was she a beauty beyond compare? What made her stand out? Why did God choose her?

We can never really know for sure this side of eternity. Yet if we read the story carefully, we may discover some vital clues.

It happened on an ordinary day . . .

> God sent the angel Gabriel to Nazareth, a town in Galilee, to a virgin pledged to be married to a man named Joseph, a descendant of David. The virgin's name was Mary. The angel went to her and said, "Greetings, you who are highly favored! The Lord is with you."[1]

It was shocking, really. We've grown accustomed to reading accounts of the supernatural in Scripture. We take it for granted: That's how things happened in those days. At first glance we don't realize just how extraordinary this moment truly was for Mary. When we turn from the Old Testament to the New Testament, we barely flip a page in our Bibles—two at most. Yet those two pages represent four hundred years. Years of silence, when God said nothing. The people eagerly awaited the fulfillment of God's promise. They looked for the coming of their Deliverer—the Messiah—the Anointed One. But years passed. Decades passed. *Centuries* passed. And nothing happened. There were no visions, no prophecies, no miracles—nothing.

Some grew tired of waiting. They gave up, bitterly concluding that God had forsaken them. Some tried to bring about their own deliverance through religious or political reform. Others simply got caught up in the dailiness of living. They had jobs to do, bills to pay, kids to raise. They were too busy for what must have seemed like fairy tales or wishful thinking. Nothing even remotely miraculous had ever happened in their lifetime—or their parents' or grandparents' or great-grandparents' lifetime. It was as hard for them to believe the supernatural stories of the Old Testament as it is for us today. Somehow it just didn't seem real. But a remnant remained faithful. A few watched and waited. And waited. And waited.

They had no idea what God was about to accomplish in their midst.

When the fullness of time had come, God sent forth his Son.[2]

Mary was a young woman, a teenager, engaged to be married. She stood at the threshold, full of hopes and dreams for her future. Like any bride-to-be, she spent most of her time preparing for her upcoming wedding. When the angel appeared, he brought a message that would change her life forever.

Mary was greatly troubled at his words and wondered what kind of greeting this might be. But the angel said to her, "Do not be afraid,

*Mary, you have found favor with God. You
will be with child and give birth to a son, and
you are to give him the name Jesus. He will be
great and will be called the Son of the Most
High. The Lord God will give him the throne
of his father David, and he will reign over
the house of Jacob forever; his kingdom will
never end."*[3]

Ever since God's promise
to Eve in the Garden of
Eden, women down through
the ages had wondered if
perhaps they might be the
one chosen to bear the
Messiah. To the faithful, it
was a sacred dream, a cher-
ished hope, a coveted honor. It
hardly seemed possible to Mary, but
the angel said it was so: God had chosen her. From
now on, all generations would call her blessed.

What an awesome privilege! What an incredible responsibility!

At that moment Mary could not have imagined all that would entail. She asked a very natural question: "How can this be?" But we can tell from the angel's gentle reply that it was not asked in doubt or skepticism.

> *"The Holy Spirit will come upon you, and the*
> *power of the Most High will overshadow you.*
> *So the holy one to be born will be called the*
> *Son of God."*[4]

With Zechariah, it was a different story. Earlier Gabriel had appeared to the priest in the temple, where he was burning incense before the Lord. The Scripture tells us that Zechariah was a righteous man who had served the Lord faithfully for many years. Sadly, he and his wife Elizabeth remained childless, despite their fervent prayers for a family. That day Gabriel brought fantastic news:

"Your prayer has been heard. Your wife Elizabeth will bear you a son . . . he will be filled with the Holy Spirit even from birth. Many of the people of Israel will he bring back to the Lord their God."[5]

How did Zechariah respond to this news? He didn't believe the angel. Face to face with a divine messenger, a supernatural angelic being, Zechariah demanded to know how this could possibly be. He protested that he and Elizabeth were too old to have children. Listen to how the angel thundered back:

"I am Gabriel. I stand in the presence of God, and I have been sent to speak to you and to tell you this good news. And now you will be silent and not able to speak until the day this happens, because you did not believe my words."[6]

When it was her turn, Mary asked the same question—she worded it almost exactly the same way. And yet it was completely different. Her heart was different. Mary didn't demand a sign—some sort of proof—or additional confirmation. She voiced no complaint at the total disruption of her life. She knew now that things would not turn out the way she had planned at all. But in her heart there was no resistance, no rebellion. Just sweet, simple submission—complete surrender to the will of God.

"Behold the handmaid of the Lord; be it unto me according to thy word."[7]

In essence, Mary told the angel that God could use her in any way He chose—because she was a willing vessel, fully available to Him. How that must have blessed the heart of God! No wonder He chose this precious young woman to be the mother of His Son.

It would not be easy. To whom much is given, much is required. Mary would have to face the pointed questions and fearful doubts of her friends and family—not to mention her incredulous fiancé. Had God not spoken to Joseph later, he might have broken their engagement. He could have accused her of committing adultery, a crime punishable by death. When it became evident that Mary had been pregnant long before her wedding day, she would endure nasty rumors, snide comments, and scornful looks. But having her name dragged through the mud—her reputation ruined—was nothing compared to the agony she would experience as the mother of the Man born to die for the sins of the world. This was one son who would not grow up to take over the family business, settle down with a sweet girl, and fill his mother's arms with adorable grandchildren.

When her miracle baby—the Child of Promise—was dedicated at the temple, the prophet Simeon warned Mary:

> *"This child is destined to cause the falling and rising of many in Israel, and to be a sign that will be spoken against, so that the thoughts of many hearts will be revealed. And a sword will pierce your own soul too."*[8]

Mary was there when Jesus began His earthly ministry. She witnessed the highs and the lows. She saw how the Pharisees hated Him, how in their jealousy they sought to destroy Him. She knew that the people in their own hometown of Nazareth rejected Him—accused him of being a false prophet and tried to stone Him. She observed firsthand that many of His disciples couldn't stomach the truth, stumbled over His teachings, and eventually abandoned Him.

> *He was in the world, and though the world was made through him, the world did not recognize him. He came to that which was his own, but his own did not receive him.*[9]

Mary lived to see her Son mocked and ridiculed, spat upon, beaten with fists—and with whips. She saw His back ripped to ribbons, His brow bruised and bloody from the crown of thorns pressed into His flesh. She was there when a sword pierced His side—when He was nailed to a cross and condemned to a most brutal and humiliating death. She stood at the foot of the cross in total shock and utter disbelief. She watched Him die.

Mary was also there three days later, when the tomb was found empty, the stone rolled away. For the second time in her life, she encountered an angel. This time it was he who had a question:

"Why do you look for the living among the dead? He is not here; he has risen!"[10]

It was then that she understood. Mary was an eyewitness to His glorious resurrection. Her Son had become her Savior. The book of Acts indicates that the early church may have met in Mary's home. Bible scholars believe it was she who provided the detailed account of Jesus' birth in the Gospel of Luke. After all, Luke himself explains:

Mary treasured up all these things and pondered them in her heart.[11]

She has become the most revered, most beloved woman in the history of the world. What one of us wouldn't give anything and everything we have to be in Mary's place. To know Jesus the way she knew Jesus. To experience God the way she experienced God. To have the extraordinary privilege of being His vessel, as Mary did.

The mind-boggling truth is that we can.

Through the Holy Spirit, Mary carried the infant Jesus in her body. By that same Holy Spirit, every one of us can carry the risen Lord in our hearts. If we invite Him to, He will dwell within us and will accomplish the work of His kingdom through us.

But all too often we miss the opportunity to experience His power at work in us because we're not willing to let Him have control. We won't surrender our own plans, our own hopes and dreams. Our hearts are set on earthly things. We don't want to do anything that might jeopardize our family, our career, our reputation, or our future.

Somehow we can't bring ourselves to step out of our comfort zone. Honestly, we're afraid of pain and suffering. Unless we have all the answers up front, unless we know how everything will turn out from the start, we're reluctant to obey. We don't trust the plans God has for us. We want some sort of guarantee.

But God doesn't work that way. He requires nothing less than total surrender, unquestioning faith, and pure, wholehearted obedience. It's true that if we give our lives to Him, He may require us to undergo hardship and heartache. But He will never ask us to suffer more for Him than He has already suffered for us. And He will never give us more than His strength will enable us to bear.

There may be dark days when we feel abandoned and alone. But He has promised that He will never leave us or forsake us. His grace is sufficient. His power is made perfect in our weakness.

For everything we give up, we receive greater things. The apostle Paul said it best:

> *I once thought all these things were so very important, but I now consider them worthless because of what Christ has done. Yes, everything else is worthless when compared with the priceless gain of knowing Christ Jesus my Lord.*[12]

Knowing Jesus becomes our deepest hope, our greatest joy, our dearest love. First Corinthians 2:9 reminds us, "No eye has seen, no ear has heard, no mind has conceived what God has prepared for those who love Him."

Though she was only a teenager, barely more than a child, Mary somehow understood all of this. She recognized the blessings and rewards of unconditional obedience. She was a truly wise woman. A woman with a willing heart.

God is still looking for women with willing hearts. Women who—like Mary—will make themselves fully available to Him. If we will surrender our hearts, our hopes, our dreams, He will use us to accomplish great and mighty things.

The Magnificat—Mary's Song

"My soul praises the Lord
and my spirit rejoices in God my Savior,
for he has been mindful of the humble state
of his servant.
From now on all generations will call me blessed,
for the Mighty One has done great things for me—
holy is his name.
His mercy extends to those who fear him,
from generation to generation.
He has performed mighty deeds with his arm;
he has scattered those who are proud in their
inmost thoughts.
He has brought down rulers from their thrones
but has lifted up the humble.
He has filled the hungry with good things
but has sent the rich away empty.
He has helped his servant Israel,
remembering to be merciful
to Abraham and his descendants forever,
even as he said to our fathers."

LUKE 1:46-55

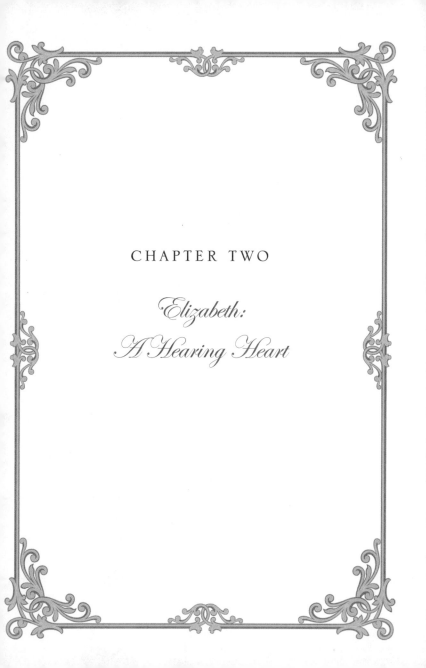

CHAPTER TWO

Elizabeth:
A Hearing Heart

2

Elizabeth:
A Hearing Heart

*"Blessed is she who has believed
that what the Lord has said to her
will be accomplished!"*

LUKE 1:45

lizabeth came from a distinguished family. She had a rich heritage. And she married well. But it wasn't enough.

> *In the time of Herod king of Judea there was
> a priest named Zechariah, who belonged to
> the priestly division of Abijah; his wife
> Elizabeth was also a descendant of Aaron. . . .
> But they had no children, because Elizabeth
> was barren.[1]*

Barren in a culture in which a woman's worth was measured by the number of children she produced. Infertile at a time when an inability to bear children was seen as a sign of God's judgment—a curse. Yet of Elizabeth and her husband, Zechariah, the Bible says,

> *Both of them were upright in the sight of God, observing all the Lord's commandments and regulations blamelessly.*[2]

Their barrenness wasn't their fault. They had done nothing to deserve this shame and disgrace. The couple prayed fervently that God would open Elizabeth's womb and give them a child. But now her childbearing years had passed, and still her arms were empty. Humanly speaking, she had every right to be hurt, angry, even bitter.

She wouldn't have been the first woman in Scripture who reacted to heartbreak this way. Rachel turned on her husband, screaming, "Give me children, or I'll die!"[3] Hannah wept inconsolably and would not eat.[4] Distraught over devastating loss, Naomi told her friends, "Do not call me Naomi [pleasant]; call me Mara [bitter], for the Almighty has dealt very bitterly with me. . . . I went away full, and the LORD has brought me back empty."[5] Similarly, overwhelmed by the financial ruin of her family, the tragic deaths of her ten children, and the extraordinary physical suffering her husband endured, Job's wife felt it was more than she could bear. She could find no comfort for herself, let alone for her poor husband. All she could suggest to Job was that he "curse God and die."[6]

The enemy of our souls knows where women are vulnerable. Since the Garden of Eden, Satan has tried to convince us that God cannot be trusted—that He is unfair, unjust, and unkind—that He deliberately withholds good things from His children out of spite. So crafty is this serpent, he uses the pain and suffering he himself has instigated as an opportunity to malign the character of God and to undermine our faith in Him.

> He [the devil] was a murderer from the beginning, not holding to the truth, for there is no truth in him. When he lies, he speaks his native language, for he is a liar and the father of lies.[7]

Those who listen to the devil's lies find themselves swept away by wave after wave of hopelessness and despair—until eventually they're drowned in his deceit. There is no doubt the enemy tried this strategy on Elizabeth. He labored long and hard to sow the seeds of bitterness in her heart, whispering his blasphemies to her day and night.

But Elizabeth refused to listen to the father of lies. She listened instead to the Holy Spirit, the Spirit of Truth. Instead of running *from* God, she ran *to* Him. Even in the midst of her heartache, she held on to hope.

> *"For I know the plans I have for you,"*
> *declares the LORD, "plans to prosper you and*
> *not to harm you, plans to give you a hope and*
> *a future. Then you will call upon me and come*
> *and pray to me, and I will listen to you. You*
> *will seek me and find me when you seek me*
> *with all your heart."*[8]

Elizabeth sought after God. She was obedient to His Word, even when she didn't understand His will. She continued to pour out her heart to Him, listening intently to Him, even when it seemed He wasn't listening to her. She chose to walk by faith, not by sight.

And then suddenly—miraculously—it happened. Long after all hope was lost, God did answer her prayers. Her obedience and faithfulness were rewarded. Zechariah had an encounter with an angel that left him speechless. Elizabeth conceived a child in her old age. And she knew without a doubt that it was the hand of God supernaturally intervening in her life.

> *"The Lord has done this for me," she said. "In these days he has shown his favor and taken away my disgrace. . . . "*[9]

Months later when her young kinswoman, Mary, arrived for an unexpected visit, Elizabeth knew why she had come. Before Mary could explain anything, Elizabeth knew. Years of suffering had brought her very near to the heart of God. She was attuned to His Spirit. She recognized the Voice she had heard so many times before. At that moment God shared a secret with Elizabeth. He revealed to her something only one other human being knew.

It was then that Elizabeth became the first human being to utter a prophetic word in the New Testament era:

> *Elizabeth was filled with the Holy Spirit. In a loud voice she exclaimed: "Blessed are you among women, and blessed is the child you will bear! But why am I so favored, that the mother of my Lord should come to me? As soon as the sound of your greeting reached my ears, the baby in my womb leaped for joy!"*[10]

What an incredible moment! Elizabeth was struck with awe and wonder, absolutely overwhelmed by God's mercy and grace. She caught a glimpse of the marvelous plan that was even now unfolding from the mind of God. She grasped the glorious truth that the long-awaited Messiah, the Anointed One, the Deliverer, had come. Israel's Strength and Consolation, the Hope of All the Earth, the Desire of Every Nation, was here at last. This same discovery caused the apostle Paul to exclaim:

Oh, the depth of the riches of the wisdom
and knowledge of God!
How unsearchable his judgments,
and his paths beyond tracing out!
"Who has known the mind of the Lord?
Or who has been his counselor?" . . .
For from him and through him and
to him are all things.
To him be the glory forever! Amen.[11]

And as if that were not enough, Elizabeth realized that the child she was carrying could not have been born any sooner. The timing of his birth was critical. He had a part to play in this divine drama. John was destined to be the greatest prophet the world had ever known.[12] He was the one who would prepare the way for the Messiah. Speaking of this miracle child, the angel Gabriel had said to Zechariah,

> *"Many of the people of Israel will he bring back to the Lord their God. And he will go on before the Lord, in the spirit and power of Elijah, to turn the hearts of the fathers to their children and the disobedient to the wisdom of the righteous—to make ready a people prepared for the Lord."*[13]

With the authority of a woman who has seen and heard and experienced God's faithfulness for herself, Elizabeth exclaimed to Mary,

"Blessed is she who has believed that what the Lord has said to her will be accomplished!"[14]

In that instant, Elizabeth took on the role of a spiritual mother or mentor to Mary. Her words brought comfort and encouragement to a young woman who felt very much alone. As she shared the truths God had spoken to her heart, Elizabeth affirmed Mary and confirmed the Word of the Lord to her. If Mary had begun to have doubts or fears, Elizabeth dispelled them with her joyous reminder of God's love and faithfulness. In response, Mary burst forth with a prophetic word of her own—a beautiful psalm of praise that would become known to all future generations as The *Magnificat*.

During the three months that Mary stayed with her, Elizabeth had many more opportunities to minister to the girl, to speak into her life, to share her testimony, and to set the kind of example the apostle Paul later referred to when he admonished the older women of the church to "train the younger women to love their husbands and children, to be self-controlled and pure, to be busy at home, to be kind, and to be subject to their husbands."[15]

Elizabeth was a perfect role model for Mary because she had a hearing heart. As she listened to the Holy Spirit, she became a woman of wisdom and maturity and depth. Her life experience had caused her to lean hard on the everlasting arms and to learn from the Lover of her soul.

In that way she is also a perfect role model for us today.

The truth is that if we live long enough, we will all experience heartache and pain and suffering. We live in a fallen world, and we cannot remain untouched by the ravages of sin. We feel the effects of the curse, and we have to deal with them. We all experience our share of physical or financial or emotional hardships. We may face the death of a dream—or the death of a loved one. We struggle as we see the people we love dealt some devastating blows.

Life is hard. Sometimes our hearts become hard too. Especially when we listen to the wrong voice—when we give ear to the father of lies. At times we allow him to confuse our hearts and minds, twist our perspective, and distort our view of God. There, in the darkness of despair, bitterness can take root and grow. We find ourselves blocking out the light of truth and hardening our hearts to the voice of God—putting a barrier between us and the one Person who truly feels our pain. The one Person who truly cares for us. The One who longs to comfort us and carry our burdens for us. The One who wants to give us hope and peace and joy in the midst of our trials, as well as the strength and courage to face each new day.

If we listen to the Holy Spirit, our hearts

remain tender and sensitive and open to God. We experience the peace that passes all understanding.[16] We live with the constant assurance of God's presence. We sense His love. We know for certain that He is in control—that there is a plan, even if we don't understand. That's what it means to live by faith, being "sure of what we hope for and certain of what we do not see."[17] We stand on the unshakable conviction expressed in Romans 8:28 (ESV):

> We know that for those who love God all things work together for good, for those who are called according to his purpose.

In time, we see the answers to our prayers, the fulfillment of His promises, the purpose behind the pain. We wouldn't exchange what God has taught us for anything in the world. We're grateful for everything we have received from Him. And we find that we have something wonderful to give. We can share with others the powerful, life-changing truths we have learned. We can befriend and mentor and encourage those who are younger in the faith, helping them on the difficult journey we all must undertake.

> *Praise be to the God and Father of our Lord Jesus Christ, the Father of compassion and the God of all comfort, who comforts us in all our troubles, so that we can comfort those in any trouble with the comfort we ourselves have received from God.*[18]

Like Elizabeth, we have to reject the lies of the enemy—keeping our hearts ever attuned to the Spirit of God, listening intently for His voice. We must hold fast to that which is true. Let our heartbreaks draw us closer to God instead of allowing them to drive us away from Him. The closer we are to Him, the more our hearts will hear, the more they will be tender and sensitive and responsive to His leading. Then we will be able to take advantage of every opportunity to encourage and affirm those around us. We will be able to speak with wisdom and authority, sharing from our own personal experience that God is worthy of our love and trust.

Zechariah's Song

"Praise be to the Lord, the God of Israel,
because he has come and has redeemed his people.
He has raised up a horn of salvation for us
in the house of his servant David
(as he said through his holy prophets of long ago),
salvation from our enemies
and from the hand of all who hate us—
to show mercy to our fathers
and to remember his holy covenant,
the oath he swore to our father Abraham:
to rescue us from the hand of our enemies,
and to enable us to serve him without fear
in holiness and righteousness before him all our days."

LUKE 1:68-75

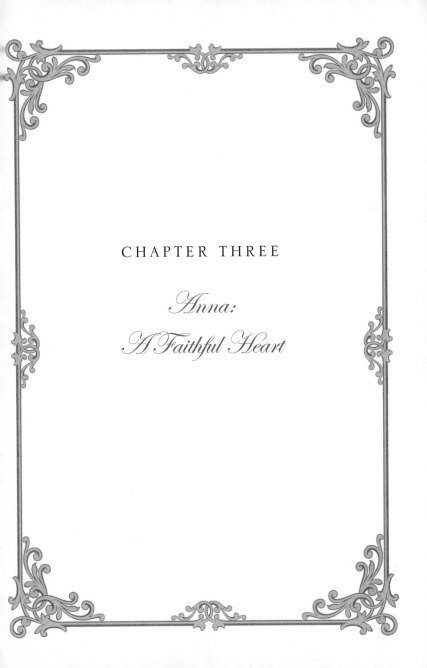

CHAPTER THREE

Anna:

A Faithful Heart

3

Anna:
A Faithful Heart

But as for me, I will always have hope;
I will praise you more and more.
My mouth will tell of your righteousness,
of your salvation all day long. . . .
Since my youth, O God, you have taught me,
and to this day I declare your marvelous deeds.
Even when I am old and gray,
do not forsake me, O God,
till I declare your power to the next generation,
your might to all who are to come.

PSALM 71:14-15, 17-18

t eighty-four, Anna was coming to the end of her life. No doubt she had already outlived most of her friends and relatives. In those days, fifty was considered a ripe old age. Anna's husband had died more than sixty years earlier, not long after they were married. There were no children to care for—and none to care for her. For some reason, contrary to what was commonly expected of her, she never remarried. And her culture didn't allow a woman to pursue a career. So Anna had a lot of time on her hands.

She could have become a gossip, a busybody, someone's dependent relative. But Anna refused to accept the traditional widow's role. She didn't spend her time living in the past and longing for the good old days. She didn't go from house to house spreading gossip and rumors and sticking her nose into other people's business. She didn't sit on the porch feeling sorry for herself, complaining to her neighbors about all her aches and pains and the problems that come with growing older. She didn't succumb to loneliness or a growing sense of futility and despair. She could have, but she didn't.

Instead, Anna devoted herself to God. She devoted herself to loving Him, worshiping Him, spending time in His presence. It's hard to imagine that any of her friends and neighbors would have understood this choice, no matter how devout they were. In that day women weren't taught to read and write, let alone study the Scriptures. They were supposed to marry and have children and manage the affairs of their household. Period. The ministry of the priesthood was not open to women. Their participation in presenting the family's yearly sacrifices was neither required nor expected. In fact, there was only one small area of the temple where women were allowed to go— the Court of Women. In the synagogues, women watched the services from behind a partition. They could listen, but they had no voice.

But the barriers society had built didn't keep Anna from hungering and thirsting after righteousness. They didn't keep her from seeking after the things of God with her whole heart. She never meant to be single, but she learned to make the most of the freedom and opportunity that gave her. Anna exemplified the kind of attitude the apostle Paul described when he wrote:

> *An unmarried woman . . . is concerned about the Lord's affairs: Her aim is to be devoted to the Lord in both body and spirit.*[1]

As the years went by, she devoted more and more of herself to Him.

> *She never left the temple but worshiped night and day, fasting and praying.*[2]

Decades passed. Anna's faithfulness and devotion gradually earned her the respect of the community. It became obvious that she had a very special relationship with God. Anna was recognized as a woman of wisdom and understanding. Even more than that, she was a "prophetess"[3]—one who speaks the word of the Lord. It was a rare distinction.

Yet there's no indication it brought her any particular prestige or influence. She didn't preside as judge over the nation of Israel as Deborah had.[4] She wasn't consulted by kings, like Huldah had been.[5] The title came without glamour, awards, or honors.

Anna lived a small life. She had a seemingly small ministry. Mostly it was just between her and the Lord. A ministry of worship, offering praise and adoration, giving glory and honor to God's name. A ministry of fasting, self-sacrifice, and self-denial—"crucifying the flesh" (Galatians

5:29) by subjugating mere physical hunger to a much deeper spiritual hunger. A ministry of prayer and intercession—crying out to God on behalf of her friends and family, the community, and the nation.

Many probably felt her time could have been better spent, that she might have been more gainfully employed. Even in this day and age, when the pursuit of spirituality is more highly regarded, Anna might not have found much support. She ought to be doing something grander, some might say, creating a program or mission or outreach, building a national or international ministry, engaging in some sort of activity that produces visible, measurable results.

Did Anna ever feel insignificant? Perhaps. Was she frustrated by the constraints of society or her circumstances? Did she wish she could take a much more active role or have a bigger ministry, with greater impact? It's possible.

But Anna had a faithful heart. She was faithful to the life and ministry to which God had called her "night and day."[6] Whether anyone else understood or approved or appreciated it or not. Whether it seemed to matter to anyone or to count for anything. Whether anyone was watching or not. Anna was steadfast, faithful.

A little thing is a little thing, but faithfulness in a little thing becomes a great thing.[7]

We do know for a fact that Anna longed for Israel's deliverance. She desperately wanted the will of God to be accomplished, all His purposes fulfilled. Anna spent her days in constant communion with Him. Day after day, year after year she eagerly sought His face, listened for His voice, waited in the presence of His Spirit.

The Scripture tells us that God honors those who honor Him.[8] Is it any wonder that when He finally appeared in the flesh, He chose to reveal Himself to this woman? He gave His servant Anna the privilege of living to see what men of old had died waiting for: the coming of the Messiah.

> *On the eighth day, when it was time to circumcise him, he was named Jesus, the name the angel had given him before he had been conceived. . . . Joseph and Mary took him to Jerusalem to present him to the Lord . . . and to offer a sacrifice in keeping with what is said in the Law of the Lord. . . .*[9]

Anna was there in the temple—where she always was—when His baby dedication took place.

> *Coming up to them at that very moment, she gave thanks to God and spoke about the child to all who were looking forward to the redemption of Jerusalem.*[10]

Her immediate response was one of thanksgiving. Gratitude overflowed from her heart. Then she shared the glorious news. She didn't keep it to herself. She told everyone who would listen about the goodness and greatness of our God. She proclaimed His salvation with all her life's breath.

If she had been twenty, Anna's words might have been easily dismissed—a grand delusion or the illusion of an idealistic youth. A sign of mental strain or instability. Perhaps a foolish young woman's attempt to gain attention and notoriety. But at eighty-four, Anna was past all of that. Her lifetime of faithful devotion could not be disregarded. Her spiritual insight and wisdom could not be denied. Now she had an audience, and it was time for her to speak. Her testimony was not unlike that of the psalmist who wrote:

> *But as for me, I will always have hope;*
> *I will praise you more and more.*
> *My mouth will tell of your righteousness,*
> *of your salvation all day long. . . .*
> *Since my youth, O God, you have taught me,*
> *and to this day I declare your marvelous deeds.*

Even when I am old and gray,
do not forsake me, O God,
till I declare your power to the next generation,
your might to all who are to come.[11]

Anna's place in Scripture takes up little more than three verses. Yet the mention of her part in the Christmas story is extremely significant. There is so much we can learn from her life, from her faithful heart.

For one thing, Anna shows us we don't have to let society's expectations or pressure from well-meaning family and friends determine the course of our lives. It's not up to them to dictate who we are or who we will become. No matter what evidence appears to the contrary, we are free to choose to answer God's call.

Whether we're married or single, our lives can have meaning and purpose. We can experience peace and contentment, regardless of our circumstances.

Sometimes a simple ministry—a quiet life of daily obedience—can be incredibly powerful. We may not be able to establish wildly successful programs or organizations or outreaches. We may not be able to travel overseas, preach to millions, or write best-selling books or popular praise songs.

But each one of us can worship. Each one of us can fast and pray. Each one of us can learn to love the Lord our God with all our heart, soul, mind, and strength.[12] We can minister to God Himself by devoting ourselves to Him, loving Him.

Anna teaches us that no matter how old we get, we don't ever have to retire from our walk with God. We can grow better instead of bitter, counting our blessings rather than our heartaches. While we have life and breath, we can proclaim God's faithfulness to the next generation, His might to all who are to come.

In *Each New Day*, 25th Anniversary Edition, Holocaust survivor Corrie ten Boom said, "I asked a parachutist, 'How did you feel when you jumped from the airplane with a parachute on your back for the first time?' He answered, 'There was only one thought: It works, it works!'"

Corrie continued, "What does it mean to go through life with Jesus? I can answer from experience, 'It works, it works!'"

As Anna discovered, this is the incredible privilege we have when we have walked with God for any length of time. We can tell others from experience that "It works!" We can tell our friends and neighbors, our children and grandchildren, our nieces and nephews, the members of our church and our community. We can share the good news with anyone who has ears to hear.

We can testify to the power of God at work in our own lives. We can demonstrate the beauty of a faithful, devoted heart. We can learn to walk with God all the days of our lives. Then, like Anna, we will stand before the Lord and hear Him say:

> "Well done, good and faithful servant. You have been faithful over a little; I will set you over much. Enter into the joy of your master."[13]

The Promise Fulfilled

The people walking in darkness have seen a great light;
on those living in the land of the shadow of death
a light has dawned. . . .
For to us a child is born,
to us a son is given,
and the government will be on his shoulders.
And he will be called
Wonderful Counselor, Mighty God,
Everlasting Father, Prince of Peace.
Of the increase of his government and peace
there will be no end.
He will reign on David's throne and over his kingdom,
establishing and upholding it with justice
and righteousness
from that time on and forever.
The zeal of the LORD Almighty will accomplish this.

ISAIAH 9:2, 6-7

Conclusion

Conclusion

This is the way the holy women of the past
who put their hope in God
used to make themselves beautiful.

1 PETER 3:5

The three Wise Women—Mary, Elizabeth, and Anna—were three very different women, in different ages and stages of life. They had their own unique personalities, their own strengths and weaknesses. None of them was perfect. Despite how artists have depicted them, they had no time to sit in state, with serene otherworldly expressions on their faces and haloes around their heads. They were real women with real lives—real responsibilities and real problems. They had their struggles, their doubts, and their

CHRISTIN DITCHFIELD

fears. There were times when they didn't understand what God was doing in their lives.

But regardless of their circumstances, these women chose to fear the Lord, to reverence Him, to trust Him. This made them wise. All three of them offered themselves as "living sacrifices, holy and pleasing to God."[1] They cultivated that "gentle and quiet spirit, which is of great worth to God."[2] This made them beautiful. Just as the Wise Men followed the star, we can follow the shining examples of these godly women today.

The Scripture tells us that when the Wise Men saw the infant Jesus, they rejoiced and bowed down and worshiped Him. Then they opened their treasures and presented Him with gifts—gold, frankincense, and myrrh.

As we read the story or see it reenacted in countless Nativity scenes and Christmas pageants, it moves us deeply. Especially when we reflect on the reality that the Lord God Almighty, Jesus

* 68 *

Christ, left the majesty of Heaven. He humbled Himself and made Himself nothing.[3] He became a tiny, helpless baby—born in a stable, of all places! They "laid him in a manger; because there was no room for them in the inn."[4]

No room for the Son of God. No royal fanfare to announce His birth. No thunderous applause.

How we wish we could have been there to welcome Him, to make a place for Him. How we wish we could comfort Him against a cold, hard, uncaring world—and the painful path that lay before Him, the journey to the cross. When we think about what it cost Him—the magnitude of His sacrifice—we can't help but be filled with awe and wonder. We wish we could express the depths of our love and gratitude—that we could shower Him with gifts, as the Wise Men did.

But what could we possibly give Him? He Himself is the very first Christmas present, the greatest Gift of all. Our most prized possessions pale in comparison. Our worldly gifts are of little use to us, let alone the God of the Universe. How could anything we have to offer hold any significance in the light of all He has done for us?

What did the three Wise Women have to give?

A willing heart. A hearing heart. A faithful heart.

These are gifts we, too, can bring to lay before the newborn King. Hearts that are willing to surrender their own hopes and dreams and make themselves fully available to Him. Hearts that are ever attuned to His Spirit, listening to His voice and walking in obedience to His Word. Hearts that are faithful in things great and small.

These gifts take time to cultivate. They require sacrifice, dedication, devotion. They show our love and gratitude to God. They bring great honor to Him.

Nineteenth-century poet Christina Rossetti captured this truth so beautifully in this familiar Christmas hymn ("In the Bleak Midwinter"):

THE THREE WISE WOMEN

In the bleak midwinter, frosty wind made moan,
Earth stood hard as iron, water like a stone;
Snow had fallen, snow on snow, snow on snow,
In the bleak midwinter, long ago.

Our God, heaven cannot hold Him, nor earth sustain;
Heaven and earth shall flee away
when He comes to reign.
In the bleak midwinter a stable place sufficed
The Lord God Almighty, Jesus Christ.

What can I give Him, poor as I am?
If I were a shepherd, I would bring a lamb;
If I were a Wise Man, I would do my part;
Yet what I can I give Him: give my heart.

Notes

CHAPTER 1

1. Luke 1:26-28.
2. Galatians 4:4, ESV.
3. Luke 1:29-33.
4. Luke 1:35.
5. Luke 1:13, 15-16.
6. Luke 1:19-20.
7. Luke 1:38, KJV.
8. Luke 2:34-35.
9. John 1:10-11.
10. Luke 24:5-6.
11. Luke 2:19.
12. Philippians 3:7-8, NLT.

CHAPTER 2

1. Luke 1:5, 7.
2. Luke 1:6.
3. Genesis 30:1.

4. 1 Samuel 1:7.

5. Ruth 1:20-21, ESV.

6. Job 2:9.

7. John 8:44.

8. Jeremiah 29:11-13.

9. Luke 1:25.

10. Luke 1:42-44.

11. Romans 11:33-36.

12. Luke 7:28.

13. Luke 1:16-17.

14. Luke 1:45.

15. Titus 2:4-5.

16. Philippians 4:7.

17. Hebrews 11:1.

18. 2 Corinthians 1:3-4.

CHAPTER 3

1. 1 Corinthians 7:34.

2. Luke 2:37.

3. Luke 2:36.

4. Judges 4:4.

5. 2 Chronicles 34:22.

6. Luke 2:37.

7. Often attributed to J. Hudson Taylor.

8. Matthew 10:32.

9. Luke 2:21-24.

10. Luke 2:38.

11. Psalm 71:14-15, 17-18.

12. Mark 12:30.

13. Matthew 25:21, ESV.

CONCLUSION

1. Romans 12:1.

2. 1 Peter 3:4.

3. Philippians 2:6-7.

4. Luke 2:7, KJV.

Acknowledgments

To the countless women who have opened their hearts to me and given me the privilege of sharing my heart with them, as together we have celebrated the Reason for the Season at Christmas brunches and banquets through the years. May we always remember that just as wise men still seek him, wise women still seek him too!

To Lee Hough, Tom Neven, and Steve Laube, whose enthusiasm for the message of this book greatly encouraged me to pursue its publication.

To Geoff Dennis, Bill Jensen, Marvin Padgett, Ted Griffin, and everyone at Crossway who caught the vision and helped bring it together so beautifully.

To my friends and family for their constant love and encouragement and support. Thank you for seeing my heart—the woman I long to be—and believing in me even as I continue to be a work in progress.

CHRISTIN DITCHFIELD is the host of the syndicated radio program "Take It To Heart!"®—heard daily on stations across the United States, Canada, and Central and South America. Using real-life stories, rich word pictures, biblical illustrations, and touches of humor, she calls believers to enthusiastically seek after God, giving them practical tools to help deepen their personal relationship with Christ.

A popular conference speaker and author of more than forty books, Christin has also written dozens of tracts for Good News Publishers, including *Under Attack* (about 9/11) and *The Passion of Jesus Christ*, each of which has sold more than a million copies worldwide. Her articles have appeared in numerous national and international magazines, including *Focus on the Family*, *Today's Christian Woman*, *Sports Spectrum*, and *Power for Living*.

You may contact Christin at:

Take It To Heart Ministries

P.O. Box 1000

Osprey, FL 34229

www.TakeItToHeartRadio.com